THE STATUTES OF KILKENNY

THE STATUTES OF KILKENNY

LIONEL OF ANTWERP

Copyright 2021 by Dalcassian Press

All rights reserved. No part of this book may be reproduced in any manner whatsoever without written permission except in the case of brief quotations embodied in critical articles and reviews.

No part of this publication may be reproduced, distributed, or transmitted in any form or by any means, including photocopying, recording, or other electronic or mechanical methods, without the prior written permission of the publisher, except in the case of brief quotations embodied in critical reviews and certain other non-commercial uses permitted by copyright law. For permission requests, write to Dalcassian Press at admin@thescriptoriumproject.com

Translator: Curtin, D.P. (1985-)

ISBN: 979-8-3492-1700-5 (Paperback)
ISBN: 979-8-3492-1701-2 (eBook)
Library of Congress Control Number:

Printed by Ingram Content Group, 1 Ingram Blvd, La Vergne, Tennessee
First Printing 2021, Dalcassian Press, Wilmington, DE

This work is part of a series produced in association with the Scriptorium Project and its community of scholars and translators.
Please visit our website at: www.thescriptoriumproject.com

INTRODUCTION

By: D.P. Curtin

 Civil documents from Ireland, outside of the limits of the city of Dublin, are rare during the medieval period. Certainly, some church synods survive, as well as a handful of texts that make up the corpus of the Irish annals. However, the Statutes of Kilkenny represent a changing tide of the history of Ireland, as legal and parliamentary documents become paramount. This is largely a function of their necessity to the Anglo-Irish ruling class, who had begun to feel the pinch that all colonial powers feel when they recognize that they are vastly outnumbered by the native population.

 For the unfamiliar, the Statutes of Kilkenny were a series of laws enacted in 1365 during the reign of King Edward III of England, while he was residing under the title of 'Lord of Ireland'. They were formulated at the Parliament of Kilkenny, a significant gathering of the English settlers and the Irish in medieval Ireland, held at Kilkenny, a town in the province of Leinster, where representatives of the Anglo-Norman ruling class met with some regularity. The ruling nobles and gentry had been imported to Ireland about two centuries prior with the purchase and conquest of Ireland under Henry II. Since that time Norman power and cultural influence had waned, in England, but also more definitively in Ireland. The statutes, tellingly composed in Law French, were a direct response to the increasing influence of native Irish customs, culture, and language among the Anglo-Irish population, which threatened the English crown's control over Ireland.

 The English Crown, particularly concerned with maintaining its authority in Ireland, sought to prevent the growing integration of the Anglo-Irish aristocracy with the native Irish population, and with the surviving Gaelic gentry, which still posed a considerable political and military threat. At the time, many of the Anglo-Irish lords, who had been settled in Ireland for several generations, were adopting Irish ways of life, customs, and the language itself. They spoke the Irish tongue freely in English colonial institutions, intermarried with native Irish families, and increasingly followed Irish customs and law (*the Brehon*), which the English Crown viewed as a challenge to its civil control in the nation.

One of the primary aims of the Statutes of Kilkenny was to reinforce English laws and customs among the Anglo-Irish settlers. The statutes prohibited Anglo-Irish people from adopting Irish traditions, including the use of the Irish language and the practice of intermarriage with the native Irish people. These measures were designed to preserve the English identity of the settler community and prevent further cultural assimilation. To some degrees these statutes remained in effect until the latter half of the twentieth century, wherein English cultural institutions were slowly brought into the fold of Irish Society. Similarly, the native Irish, following these edicts, sought to firmly reject the English civil and cultural authority, and would continue to reject it for several coming centuries. This was at least particularly a mutual cultural excommunication, and would continue on for centuries, as best evidenced with the anathema levied on any Fenian who sought to find education through Trinity College Dublin, an Elizabethan institution founded for the education of the English Colonial Ruling Class. This anathema was not lifted until 1971.

These statutes also sought to address political and military concerns, which were a prominent feature of Anglo-Norman society. They outlawed the practice of "Irishry," where Anglo-Irish lords would ally themselves with native Irish clans, which often undermined English civil authority. The statutes attempted to restrict the ability of Anglo-Irish lords to grant lands to the native Irish or to employ them in positions of courtly or legal power, aiming to ensure that English influence remained predominant.

STATUTES OF KILKENNY

Statute of the Fortieth Year of King Edward III

Enacted in a parliament held in Kilkenny, A.D. 1367, before Lionel Duke of Clarence, Lord Lieutenant of Ireland.

Whereas at the conquest of the land of Ireland, and for a long time after, the English of the said land used the English language, mode of riding and apparel, and were governed and ruled, both they and their subjects called Betaghes, according to the English law, in which time God and holy Church, and their franchises according to their condition were maintained *and themselves lived* in *due* subjection; but now many English of the said land, forsaking the English language, manners, mode of riding, laws and usages, live and govern themselves according to the manners, fashion, and language of the Irish enemies; and also have made divers marriages and alliances between themselves and the Irish enemies aforesaid; whereby the said land, and the liege people thereof, the English language, the allagiance due to our lord the king, and the English laws there, are put in subjection and decayed, and the Irish enemies exalted and raised up, contrary to reason; our lord the king considering the mischiefs aforesaid, in the consequence of the grievous complaints of the commons of his said land, called to his parliament held at Kilkenny, the Thursday next after the day of Cinders *Ash Wednesday* in the fortieth year of his reign, before his well-beloved son, Lionel Duke of Clarence, his lieutenant in his parts of Ireland, to the honour of God and His glorious Mother, and of holy Church, and for the good government of the said land, and quiet of the people, and for the better observation of the laws, and punishment of evils doers there, are ordained and established by our said lord the king, and his said lieutenant, and our lord the king's counsel there, which the assent of the archbishops, bishops, abbots and priors (as to what appertains to them to assent to), the earls, barons, and others the commons of the said land, at the said parliament there being and assembled, the ordinances and articles under written, to be held and kept perpetually upon the pains contained therein.

I. First, it is ordained, agreed to, and established, that holy Church shall be free, and have all her franchises without injury, according to the franchises ordained and granted by our lord the king, or his progenitors, by *any* statute or ordinance made in England or in Ireland heretofore; and if any (which God forbid) do to the contrary, and be excommunicated by the ordinary of the place for that cause, so that satisfaction be not made to God and holy Church by the party so excommunicated, within the month after such excommunication, that then, after certificate thereupon being made, by the said ordinary, into the Chancery, a writ shall be directed to the sheriff, mayor, seneschal of franchise, or other officers of our lord the king, to take his body, and to keep him in prison without enlarging him by mainprize or bail, until satisfaction be made to God and holy Church, notwithstanding that the forty days be not passed; and that no prohibition from Chancery be henceforth granted in any suit against the franchise of holy Church; saving at all times the right for our lord the king, and of his crown; so that the franchises of holy Church be not overturned or injured; and in case that by suggestion of the party prohibition be granted, that as soon as the articles of franchise shall be shown by the ordinary in the Chancery, a consultation shall thereupon be granted to him without delay.

II. Also, it is ordained and established, that no alliance by marriage, gossipred, fostering of children, concubinage or by amour, nor in any other manner, be hencefoth made betweeen the English and Irish of one part, or of the other part; and that no Englishman, nor other person, being at peace, do give or sell to any Irishman, in time of peace or war, horses or armour, nor any manner of victuals in time of war; and if any shall do to the contrary, and thereof be attainted, he shall have judgment of life and member, as a traitor to our lord the king.

III. Also, it is ordained and established, that every Englishman do use the English language, and be named by an English name, leaving off entirely the manner of naming used by the Irish; and that every Englishman use the English custom, fashion, mode of riding and apparel, according to his estate; and if any English, or Irish living amongst the English, use the Irish language amongst themselves, contrary to the ordinance, and therof be attainted, his lands and tenements, if he have any, shall be seized into the hands of his immediate lord, until he shall come to one of the places of our lord the king, and find sufficient surety to adopt and use the English language, and then he shall have restitution of his said lands or tenements, his body shall be taken by any of the officers of our lord the king, and commited to the next gaol, there to remain until he, or some other in his name, shall find sufficient surety in the manner aforesaid: And that no Englishman who shall have the value of one hundred pounds of land or of rent by the year, shall ride otherwise than on a saddle in the English fashion; and he that shall do to the contrary, and shall be thereof attainted, his horse shall be forfeited to our lord the king, and his body shall be committed to prison, until he pay a fine according to the king's pleasure for the contempt aforesaid; and also, that beneficed persons of holy Church, living amongst the English, shall have the issues of their benefices until they use the English language in the manner aforesaid; and they shall have respite in order to learn the English language, and to provide saddles, between this and the feast of Saint Michael next coming.

IV. Also, whereas diversity of government and different laws in the same land cause difference in allegiance, and disputes among the people; it is agreed and established, that no Englishman, having disputes with any other Englishman, shall henceforth make caption, or take pledge, distress or vengeance against any other, whereby the people may be troubled, but that they shall sue each other at the common law; and that no Englishman be governed in the termination of their disputes by March law nor Brehon law, which reasonably ought not to, be called law, being a bad custom; but they shall be governed, as right is, by the common law of the land, as liege subjects of our lord the king; and if any do to the contrary, and thereof be attainted, he shall be taken and imprisoned and adjudged as a traitor; and that no difference of allegiance shall henceforth be made between the english born in born in Ireland, and the English born in England, by calling them English hobbe, or Irish dog, but that all be called by one, name, the English lieges of our Lord the king; and he who shall be found *doing* to the contrary, shall be punished by imprisonment for a year, and afterwards fined, at the king's pleasure; and by this ordinance it is not the intention of our Lord the king *but* that it shall be lawful for any one that he may take distress for service and rents due to them, and for damage feasant as the common law requires.

V. Also, whereas the liege people of our lord the king of his land of Ireland, or the wars of the same land cannot reasonably be controlled, unless the sale of victuals be reasonably regulated, it is ordained and established as to the merchandizes which are come, or shall come, to the same land by any merchants, and at whatever port, town or city they shall arrive, that before the said merchandizes.

be put up to sale, the mayor, sovereign, bailiff, or other officer who shall have care of the place where the said merchandizes shall be sold, do cause to come before them two of the most respectable and sufficient men of the said place, who meddle not in such merchandizes, and that the said mayor, seneschal, sovereign or bailiff; with the said two persons, do cause to come before them the merchants to whom the said merchandizes shall belong, and the sailors, and they shall be sworn truly to tell und show the amount of the first purchase *prime cost* of the said merchandizes, and of the expenses on them to the port, and thereupon that a reasonable price be put upon the said merchandizes by the said mayor, seneschal, bailiff or provost, and by the two discreet men aforesaid, without favour, as they may be able to vouch before our lord the king's council of these parts; and at such prices they shall be sold, without more being taken for them, upon forfeiture of the same, although the said merchandizes should have there become chargeable afterwards.

VI. Also, whereas a land, which is at war, requires that every person do render himself able to defend himself, it is ordained, and established, that the commons of the said land of Ireland, who are in the different marches at war, do not, henceforth, use the plays which men call horlings, with great sticks *and a ball* upon the ground, from which great evils and maims have arisen, to the weakening, of the defence of the said land, and other plays which men call coiting; but that they do apply and accustom themselves to use and draw bows, and throw lances, and other gentlemanlike games, whereby the Irish enemies may be the better checked by the liege people and commons of these parts; and if any do or practise the contrary, and of this be attainted, they shall be taken and imprisoned, and fined at the will of our lord the king.

VII. Also, whereas by conspiracies, confederacies, champerties, maintainors of quarrel, false swearers, retainers, sharers of damages, the liege commons of the said land in pursuit of their rights are much disturbed, aggrieved, and deprived of their inheritance; it is ordained and established, that diligent inquiry be made of such in every county, by the Justices to hold pleas in the chief place, and of their maintainors, and that due and expeditious execution be had against those who shall be attainted thereof, according to the form of the Statute in this respect made in England, without fine or redemption to be taken of them, that others may, by such speedy execution, be deterred from doing or maintaining such horrible acts contrary to law, in grievance of the said liege commons: and that, thereupon, the archbishops and bishops of the said land, each within his diocese, shall have letters patent of our lord the king, from his chancery of Ireland, to inquire of the articles aforesaid when they think fit; and, thereupon, according to the law of holy Church to proceed against them by censures, and to certify into the said Chancery the names *of those* who shall be before them found guilty thereof, so that our lord the king, to the honour of God and the holy Church, the government of his laws, and the preservation of his said people, may inflict due punishment for the same.

VIII. Also, whereas, of right, no lay person whatsoever ought to meddle with tithes, or any spiritual goods, against the will of the governors of the Church, to whom tithes or such spiritual goods belong, it is ordained and established, that no man, great or little, shall interfere with or take by sale, in any other manner, the tithes appertaining to holy Church or religion, by extortion or menace, nor at a less price than they may be sold at to another, against the will of him to whom the said tithes belong, and he who does to the contrary, and hereof shall be attainted, shall make restitution to him who shall be aggrieved, if he will complain, of the double of the said price, and make fine at the king's pleasure.

IX. Also, whereas *persons guilty of* disobedience to God and holy Church, and put out of the communion of Christians, cannot, nor ought, of right, to be received to the favour of our lord the king, or to the communion of his officers; it is ordained and established, that when the archbishops, bishops and other prelates of holy Church, have excommunicated, interdicted or fulminated the censures of holy Church against any English person or Irish, for reasonable cause, at the request of our lord the king, or ex-officio, or at the suit of the party, that after the notification of these censures shall come to our lord the king, nor into communion or alliance with his ministers, nor to maintenance in their error by any of the liege people, until they shall have made satisfaction to God and holy Church, and shall be restored as the law of holy Church requires; and if a maintainor of such excommunicated person be found and attainted against the ordinance aforesaid, he shall be taken and imprisoned, and fined at the king's will.

X. Also, whereas divers wars have often heretofore been commenced and not continued, nor brought to a good termination, but by the party taking from the enemy at their departure a small tribute, whereby the said enemies were and are the more emboldened to renew the war; it is agreed and established, that any war which shall be commenced hereafter, shall be undertaken by the council of our lord the king, by the advice of the lords, commons, and inhabitants of the marches of the county where the war shall arise; and shall be continued, and finished and supplied, by their advice and counsel; so that the Irish enemies shall not be admitted to peace, until they shall be finally destroyed, or shall make restitution fully of the costs and charges expended upon that war by their default and rebellion, and make reparation to those by whom the said charges and costs were incurred, and moreover, pay a fine for the contempt at the king's will; and in case that hostages be taken and given to our lord the king, or to his officers, for keeping the peace, by any of the Irish, that, if they shall renew the war against the form of their peace, execution of their said hostages shall without delay or favour be made, according to the ancient customs of the said land in such case used.

XI. Also for the better maintaining of peace, and doing right, as well to the Irish enemies being at peace as to the English, it is ordained and established, that if any Irishman, being at peace, by borrowing, or purchase of merchandize, or in any other manner, become debtor to an English, or Irishman being at peace, that for this cause no other Irish person belonging to him, under him, or in subjection to him, nor his goods, shall be seized nor ransomed for such debt; but his remedy shall be against the principal debtor, as the law requires. Let him be well advised to give his merchandise to such person as he can have recovery from.

XII. Also, it is ordained and established, that in every peace to be henceforth made, between our lord the king and his liege English of the one part, and the Irish of the other part, in every march of the land, there shall be comprised the point which follows, that is to say, that no Irishman shall pasture or occupy the lands belonging to English, or Irish being at peace, against the will of the lords of the said lands; and if they so do, that it shall be lawful for the said lords to lead with them to their pound the said beasts so feeding *or* occupying their said lands, in name of a for their rent and their damages, so that the beasts be not divided nor scattered as heretofore has been done; but that they be kept altogether as they were taken, in order to deliver them to the party in case that he shall come to make satisfaction to the lords of the said lands reasonably, according to their demand; and in case any one shall divide or separate from each other the beasts so taken, he shall be punished as a robber and disturber of the peace of our lord the king; and if any Irish rise by force to the rescue of those reasonably taken, that it is lawful for the said English to assist themselves by strong hand, without being impeached in the court of our lord the king on this account; and that no Englishman do take any distress upon any Irishman of any part between this and the Feast of St.

Michael next to come; so that the Irish of every part may be warned in the meantime.

XIII. Also, it it is ordained that no Irishman of the nations of the Irish be admitted into any cathedral or collegiate church by provision, collation, or presentation of any person, nor to any benefice of Holy Church, amongst the English of the land; and that if any be admitted, instituted or inducted, into such benefice, it be held for void, and the king, shall have the presentation of the said benefice for that avoidance, to whatever person the advowson of such benefice may belong, saving their right to present or make collation to the said benefice when it shall be vacant another time.

XIV. Also, it is ordained and established that no religious house which is situate amongst the English *be it exempt or not,*, shall henceforth receive any Irishmen to their profession, but may receive Englishmen without taking into consideration whether they be born in England or in Ireland; and that any that shall act otherwise, and thereof shall be attainted, their temporalties shall be seized into the hands of our lord the king, so to remain at his pleasure; and that no prelates of holy Church shall receive any [...] to any orders without the assent and testimony of his lord, given to him under his seal.

XV. Also, whereas the Irish agents who come amongst the English, spy out the secrets, plans, and policies of the English, whereby great evils have often resulted; it is agreed and forbidden, that any Irish agents, that is to say, pipers, story-tellers, bablers, rimers, mowers, nor any other Irish agent shall come amongst the English, and that no English shall receive or make gift to such; and that shall do so, and be attainted, shall be taken, and imprisoned, as well the Irish agents as the English who receive or give them any thing, and after that they shall make fine at the king's will; and the instruments of their agency shall forfeit to our lord the king.

XVI. Also, it is agreed and assented, that no man's escape henceforth shall be adjudged against any, by any inquest of office, before the party against whom the escape ought to be adjudged, be himself put to answer or acknowledge the fact, or plea of record, although heretofore, it has been otherwise practised.

XVII. Also it is agreed and assented that no man, of what estate or condition he be, upon forfeiture of life or of members, shall keep kerns, hoblers nor idlemen in land at peace, to aggrive the loyal people of our lord the king; but that he who will have such shall keep them in the march at his own expense, without taking anything from any person against his will: and if it happen that any man, whether a kern or any other, shall take any manner of victuals or other goods of any other against his will, hue and cry shall be raised against him, and he shall be taken and committed to gaol if he will surrender himself; and if not, but he rise to make resistance by force, so that he will not suffer the attachment, it shall be done to him as to open robbers; and such manner of taking shall be considered a robbery; and in case such malefactors fly from the attachment, so that no man can take them, then his lord or leader shall answer for him, and shall make satisfaction to the party who has been damaged; and if he shall have made satisfaction to the party, the king shall end the flight against him as well for himself as for the party; and those who do not rise at such hue and cry shall be holden and punished as maintainors of felons; and if any man keep or maintain kerns, hoblers, or idlemen, otherwise than is abovesaid, he shall be in judgment of life and members, and his lands und tenements shall be forfeited.

XVIII. Also, that it shall be proclaimed that all those who are now idlemen, and are willing to take land of the king, shall come to the Lord duke, lieutenant of our lord the king of Ireland, the chancellor or treasurer of the king, and shall take waste lands of the king, in fee or to farm, and if they wish to take of other lords, they shall come to them, or to their seneschal, in like manner. And that no marcher, or other shall hold parley or alliance with any Irish or English who shall be against peace, without leave of the Court, or in the presence of the sheriff of our lord the king, or the wardens of the peace, that they may see that such parley or alliance is for common and not for particular benefit; and he who does to the contrary, shall be imprisoned, and make fine at the kings will.

XIX. Also, it is ordained and established, that if any of the lineage, or of the adherents or retainers of any chieftain of English lineage, within the land of Ireland, whom the said chieftain can correct, shall commit any trespass or felony, the said chieftain, after he shall have had notice thereof; shall cause the said malefactor to be taken and commit him to the next gaol, there to remain until he shall be delivered by law; and if the said chieftain shall not do so, that his body shall be taken for the said malefactor, and detained in prison until the body of the malefactor be given up to the court of our lord the King, to be amenable to justice as is above said; and nevertheless the said chieftain for the contempt shall be fined at the king's will, and make satisfaction to the party so aggrieved.

XX. Also, it is agreed and assented that one peace and war be throughout the entire land, so that if any Irish or English shall make a hostile inroad in any county, the counties surrounding them shall make war and harass them in their marches, so soon as they shall be warned by the wardens of the peace of the said county, or by the sheriff where the war shall arise; and if they shall not so do, they shall be held as maintainors of felons; and if they of the country where the war arises, suffer their marches to be laid waste by the enemy, and will not rise to check the malice of the enemy after they shall be reasonably warned by the wardens of the peace, or by the sheriff, or proclamation has been made publicly throughout the said county, that then they shall be considered as maintainors of felons.

XXI. Also, whereas divers people commit divers robberies and felonies in franchises, and fly with their goods into guildable lands, so that the officers of the franchises are unable to execute their office there, or to take the felons or their goods, but they are there with their goods received; and in like manner divers people who commit divers robberies and felonies in guildable lands, fly with their goods into franchises, so that the officers of our lord the King cannot there execute their office, nor take the felons with their goods, but they are there with their goods received: it is agreed and assented that if any officer of a franchise make pursuit after any such felon into guildable land, that those of the guildable land shall assist to take such felon, and to deliver him to said officer, together with the goods found with him, and thereupon deliver up both his body and goods to the said officer to do that which to law appertains; and that those of a franchise shall act in like manner towards the sheriff of our lord the king, or his officers that shall make pursuit after such felons, who commit felonies and fly with their goods into franchises; and if any man commit felony in one county, and fly into another county, or into a franchise, and shall remain there, that the sheriff of that county where the felony was committed shall have power to order by his precepts, the sheriffs or seneschals of the parts where the said felon remains, as well within franchises as without, to take the body of the said felon, and to send it back; and that the said sheriffs and seneschals shall be obedient each in such case to the order of the other. And if any person of guildable land or of franchise shall rise in aid of such misdoers, so that the officers cannot excecute their office on them, that they shall be considered as notorious felons as those who commit the robberies, and be punished in the same manner. And if the officers aforesaid be remiss in the execution of the orders aforesaid, and thereof be attainted, that they shall be condemned to prison, and make fine at the king's will. And it is not the intention of the King nor of the council, that, by such entry into a franchise, or order to the seneschal, the franchise shall be injured.

XXII. Also, whereas divers people enfeof their children or other strangers of their lands, and give their goods and chattels by fraud and collusion, in order to bar and delay our lord the King of his debt, and parties of their action; and also make many feofments of their lands and tenements, in order to have divers vouchers, and abate writs; it is agreed and assented that if such alienors or feoffors take the profit of the said lands and tenements after such alienations or enfeofments made, that they, notwithstanding the said feigned alienations or feofments made, shall be adjudged tenants to all the writs purchased, and that they shall not vouch any of the persons so enfeofed; and that our lord the King, and the parties, shall have execution and recovery of the lands, goods and chattels so aliened, as well as of the proper goods and chattels of the said alienors; and if it happen that any man, in purposing to levy war against the king, or to commit any felony, do enfeof any person of his land, in order to commit such felonies and treasons after the enfeofment, and if afterwards he be attainted of the treasons or felonies abovesaid, that the lands aforesaid, into whatever hands they shall come, shall be forfeited, notwithstanding the feofment, as if they were in his hand the very clay of the felony committed: and this ordenance shall have place in respect to feofments on this account, as well heretofore made as hereafter to be made.

XXIII. Also, in every county there shall be appointed four of the most substantial men of the county, to be wardens of the peace, who shall have full power to assess horsemen-at-arms, hoblers and footmen, each according to the value and quantity of his lands, goods and chattels, so that they shall be ready whensoever there shall be occasion for them, to arrest the malice of the enemy, according, to what they shall be assessed by the wardens aforesaid; and that the said wardens, after array made in manner aforesaid, shall review the said men-at-arms, hoblers, and footmen, from month to month, in a certain place in the county, where they shall see best to do the same in ease of the people: and if the said wardens shall find any rebel who will not obey their commands, they shall have power to attach them, and commit them to the next gaol, there to remain until the law shall take its course respecting them. And if the wardens of the peace shall be remiss or negligent in performing their duty, and thereof be attainted, then they shall be taken and imprisoned, and make fine at the king's will. And if any one so chosen a warden shall refuse to receive the king's commission, he shall be taken and imprisoned, and his lands seized into the hands of our lord the king, and so shall remain until the king shall have otherwise ordained concerning him; and the said wardens shall make oath legally to perform their duty in the manner abovesaid.

XXIV. Also, it is ordained that the marshals of the one bench, and of the other, and within franchises do not henceforth take for their fee more than they take in England; that is to say five pence, as it has been proved to the council that they do in England, according to the Statute in England in this behalf provided; and this after a man shall be acquitted or convicted, and finally delivered out of the court, and not before; and if they do to the contrary, and thereof be attainted, their bailiwicks, shall be seized into the king's hand at the complaint of him who shall be aggrieved contrary to this Statute, and shall moreover make satisfaction to those who shall be so damaged by them, and be detained in prison until their satisfaction be made. Also, that the marshal of the Exchequer shall only take half a mark every term while a man remains in his custody for arrears of account or for the king's debt; and he who does to the contrary, and thereof shall be attainted, shall suffer as is abovesaid. And that no constable of castles, within franchise or without, shall take of any prisoner put into his custody for his fee but only five pence, except the constable of the Castle of Dyvelin, which is the king's chief castle in Ireland, by reason that it has been proved to the council that he is entitled to take more, and from ancient time has done so; and he who does otherwise, and thereof shall be attainted, his office of constable shall be seized into the hands of the king, and he who shall have acted so shall be taken and imprisoned until he make satisfaction to the party, and pay a fine to the king. And that the marshals or constables aforesaid within franchises or without, shall not put the prisoners which they have in their custody to distress and severity of punishment, for the purpose of obtaining individual profit or suit; and if they shall do so they shall be taken and detained in prison until they shall have rendered double to him from whom they have received such wrongful profit, and shall moreover pay a fine to the king. And hereupon writs shall be issued to every place of the land where there is a marshal or constable, as well within franchise as without, commanding the justice of each place, and also the treasurer and barons of the Exchequer, to cause charge to be given to the marshal of their place, that they do not take of any person otherwise than as aforesaid; and to inquire from them from time to time respecting those who do the contrary, and to punish them in the form above said.

XXV. Also, it is ordained and established that if any man commit felony, and shall fly, or be attainted by outlawry, or in any other way, whereby his goods and chattels shall be forfeited to the king, that the sheriffs of the same county where the said felonies are committed shall seize the said goods and chattels into the king's hands, into whatever hands they may have afterwards come; and that our lord the king shall be answered in respect thereof in their accounts; and if they put such goods and chattels into any custody, they shall put them into such custody, that they will be able to answer for them, and that such shall not be exchanged, as it has been practised before this time.

XXVI. Also it is ordained that if truce or peace be made by the justices, or wardens of the peace, or the sheriff, between English and Irish, and they shall be broken by any English, and thereof be attainted, he shall be taken and put in prison until satisfaction be made by him to those who shall be disturbed *or* injured by that occasion, and he shall moreover make fine at the King's will; and if there is not wherewith to make restitution to those who shall be injured, he shall remain in perpetual confinement. And such wardens and sheriffs shall have power to inquire concerning those who shall have broken the peace.

XXVII. Also, it is ordained that if dispute shall arise between English and English, whereby the English on one side and on the other shall gather to themselves English and Irish being at peace, there to remain to make war upon and aggrieve the other, to the great damage and destruction of the King's liege people; it is agreed and assented that no English shall be so daring as to make war with each other, or henceforward to draw away any English or Irish at peace for such purpose, and if they shall so do, and thereof be attainted, there shall be judgement of life and members, and their goods forfeited.

XXVIII. Also, it is agreed that no man of what state or condition he be, shall make any manner of disturbance against any of the officers of our Lord the King, whereby he may be unable to execute his office; and he who so does, and thereof shall be attainted, shall be taken and imprisoned, and make fine at the King's pleasure.

XXIX. Also it is ordained that no English, being common malefactors, or common robbers or barrators, shall be maintained by any of the King's court, nor by the great or little of the land, upon the peril that awaits it, that is to say, that if he be a lord of the franchise, he shall lose his franchise, and if any other person, he shall be taken and make fine at the King's pleasure.

XXX. Also, it is ordained that the chief serjeants of fees, and their attorneys, do duly execute the writs of the King, and of his sheriffs, as they ought to do; and if they shall not so do, and thereof be attainted, their bailiwicks shall be seized into the King's hands, and their bodies be sent to prison: and that henceforth they shall not lease their bailiwicks at a higher rent than anciently it was, according to what by the Statute thereupon made in England is ordained.

XXXI. Also, whereas the summonses of the Exchequer of our Lord the King, of Ireland, come to divers sheriffs and seneschals of franchise, to levy the debts of our Lord the King off divers persons in their bailiwicks; the which sheriffs and seneschals, together with the serjeants of counties and franchises do accordingly levy divers sums of the said debts off divers persons of counties *and* franchises, and do not discharge them in their accounts at the Exchequer, but excuse themselves by the serjeants of fee and their deputies, whereby the payment of the debts of our Lord the King is so retarded and delayed, and the people greatly injured, in this respect, that they are not discharged of the money that they have paid; it is agreed and assented, that when the sheriffs and seneschals of Louth, Meath, Trim, Dublin, Kildare, Catherlogh, Kilkenny, Wexford, Waterford, and Tipperary, shall come to render up their accounts before the treasurer and barons, of the issues of their bailiwicks, that the serjeants of the fee that shall be present, and the deputies of those that shall be out of the land, shall be distrained to come into the Exchequer, and there remain with the said sheriffs and seneschals, until the said sheriffs and seneschals shall have fully accounted; and if it shall so be, that the said sheriffs and seneschals can charge the said serjeants or their deputies, that they have received the King's money of any one, and have not made payment to the said sheriffs or seneschals, and they thereupon shall be attainted, their bodies shall remain in custody of the marshal, until satisfaction be made to our Lord the King, for his money, in discharge of the debtors of our Lord the King, or of the said sheriffs or seneschals, if they have wherewithal, and if not, that they shall remain in prison until they be delivered by the council, and nevertheless the sheriff and seneschals shall be charged therewith in their accounts as before. And that all debts levied by the serjeants be paid to the sheriffs by indenture made between them; so that when the said serjeants shall come on the account of the sheriff in the Exchequer, they may show their indenture, and prove from whom they have received the King's money, and from whom not. And whereas the counties of Connaught, Kerry, Cork, and Limerick, are so far from the court, that the serjeants of the said counties cannot conveniently come to the said Exchequer, to be present on the accounts of the sheriffs and seneschals of the said counties, as other serjeants do, it is agreed and assented that when one of the barons, or a clerk assigned by the treasurer and baron, shall come by the commission of the Exchequer to the parts aforesaid, in order to examine the truth, and to deny the debt of our Lord the King, the serjeants of the said counties or their deputies shall then remain with the said baron or clerk, as long as the said sheriffs and seneschals shall remain, and if it shall happen that they shall have received any part thereof from any person, without making payment to the said sheriffs or seneschals, in the manner aforesaid, that then they shall be arrested, and suffer the punishment aforesaid.

XXXII. Also, whereas the fees of sheriffs are settled by statute, and the sheriffs in the land of Ireland take in their tourns of every barony in their bailiwick, one mark yearly, and of every market town at a time, twenty shillings, ten shillings, and half a mark, to the great oppression of the people; it is agreed and assented that the aforesaid sheriffs shall hold their tourns twice in the year, that is to say, after the feast of Saint Michael, and after Easter; and that they shall take only forty pence off every barony at each tourn, however numerous the market towns or boroughs may be within the said barony: and if he be so paid by the lord of the barony, unless he be requested or invited to eat he shall take nothing; and that no clerks of the sheriffs on account of such tourn shall take any thing; and also, that from henceforth no money shall be levied out of any ploughland, nor in any other manner, on account of executing this office, except half a mark yearly as is aforesaid; and if any person shall act contrary to the ordinance aforesaid, and thereof be attainted, he shall be committed to prison, and moreover, shall render to those from whom he shall have taken any thing of this account against the said ordinance, double thereof if they will complain, and shall moreover make fine at the King's will. And that no sheriffs of franchises, who of reason ought to have certain fees from the lords of the said franchise for executing their office, shall take any thing for their tourns from the people of their bailiwicks, but shall consider themselves paid by what they shall receive from the said lords of franchises; and if they do so, and thereof be attainted, they shall suffer the same punishment.

XXXIII. Also, whereas the commons of the *said* land complain that they are in divers ways distressed by want of servants, whereof the justices appointed for labourers, are a great cause, by reason that the common labourers are for the greatest part absent, and fly out of the said land; it is agreed and assented, that, because living and victuals are dearer than they were wont to be, each labourer in his degree, according to the discretion of two of the most substantial and discreet men of the city, town, borough, village, or hamlet, in the country where he shall perform his labour, shall receive his maintenance reasonably, in gross or by the day, and if they will not do so, nor be obedient, they shall be taken before the mayor, seneschal, sovereign, provost or bailiff of the cities or towns where they are, or by the sheriff of the county, and put in prison, until the coming of the justices assigned, who will come twice in the year into every county *and* the justice of the chief place, who shall award due punishment for the same, and right to the parties who shall feel themselves aggrieved thereby. And that no labour shall pass beyond sea; and in case that he shall do so and shall return, he shall be taken and put in prison for a year, and afterwards make fine at the King's will. And moreover, writs shall be issued to the sheriffs, mayors, seneschals, sovereigns, and bailiffs, of counties, cities and towns throughout the land where the sea reaches, commanding them that they do not suffer any such passage of labourers. And it is also agreed that the commissions issued to justices of labourers in every county he repealed, and that henceforth none such be granted.

XXXIV. Also, it is agreed and established, that in maintenance of the execution of the Statutes aforesaid, two prudent men, learned in the law, having with them two of the most substantial men of the county, by the King's council associated, be assigned by commission to inquire twice a year in every county respecting, those who shall break the articles aforesaid, and to hear and determine such cases thereunder as shall come before them by indictment, or at the suit of the party, and of the different other articles which shall be contained in the said commission, according to the penalties thereof in the said statutes contained, without doing favour to any one, and to certify unto the Chancery from time to time that which by them shall have been done therein.

XXXV. Also, our lord the duke of Clarence, lieutenant of our lord the King, in Ireland, and the council of our said lord the King there, the earls, barons and commons of the land aforesaid, at this present Parliament assembled, have requested the archbishops and bishops, abbots, priors and other persons of religion, that they do cause to be excommunicated, and do excommunicate the persons contravening the statutes and ordinances aforesaid, and the other censures of holy church to fulminate against them, if any, by rebellion of heart, act against the statutes and ordinances aforementioned. And we, Thomas archbishop of Duvelin *Dublin*, Thomas archbishop of Cashel, John archbishop of Thueme *Tuam*, Thomas bishop, of Lismore and Waterford, Thomas bishop of Killalo, William bishop of Ossory, John bishop of Leighlin, and John bishop of Clon, being present in the said parliament, at the request of our said most worthy lord the Duke of Clarence, lieutenant of our lord the King, in Ireland, and the lords and commons aforesaid, against those contravening the Statutes and ordinances aforesaid, passing over the time preceding, do fulminate sentence of excommunication, and do excommunicate them by this present writing, we and each of us reserving absolution for ourselves and for our subjects if we should be in peril of death.

This work was produced in association with:

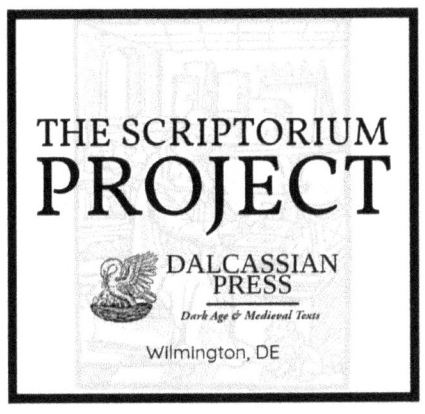

www.ingramcontent.com/pod-product-compliance
Lightning Source LLC
LaVergne TN
LVHW061049070526
838201LV00074B/5242